IMAGINE LIFE WITHOUT AFRICAN AMERICAN INVENTORS

© 2021

ALL RIGHTS RESERVED. No part of this book may be reproduced in any written, electronic, recording, or photocopying without written permission of the publisher or author. The exception would be in the case of brief quotations embodied in the critical articles or reviews and pages where permission is specifically granted by the publisher or author.

LEGAL DISCLAIMER. Although the author and publisher have made every effort to ensure that the information in this book was correct at press time, the author and publisher do not assume and hereby disclaim any liability to any party for any loss, damage, or disruption caused by errors or omissions, whether such errors or omissions result from negligence, accident, or any other cause.

Published By: Pen Legacy®

Illustration & Formatting By: India Sheana

Edited By: U Can Mark My Word Editorial Services

Library of Congress Cataloging – in- Publication Data has been applied for.

ISBN: 9781736411247

PRINTED IN THE UNITED STATES OF AMERICA.

This Book Is Dedicated To All
African-American Boys and Girls

Your Ancestors Paid The Ultimate Price For
You To Enjoy The American Dream.
Don't Take It For Granted

"Good morning, boys and girls! Happy Black History Month," Principal Imani said as the children walked into the school building.

"I wonder what project we're going to do this year," Michelle said to Marquis.

"I don't know," Marquis replied. "I hope it's something other than hearing about Martin Luther King Jr., Harriet Tubman, Malcolm X, Rosa Parks, Frederick Douglass, and Sojourner Truth.

"Right! There were way more black educators, leaders, and abolitionists than what they teach us," said Michelle.

"Good morning, class," Mr. Kentrell said, greeting his students. "I hope you're excited about this year's Black History celebration."

"I hope we're going to learn something else," Marquis responded. "There is more to our history than slavery and the civil rights movement. African Americans have contributed to this country more than what our textbooks tell us."

Smiling, Mr. Kentrell replied, "You are absolutely right. We have contributed to and broken barriers in education, sports, entrepreneurship, politics, entertainment, and inventions."

"So can we learn about those people, Mr. Kentrell?" Marquis asked.

"I'm happy you asked, Marquis," Mr. Kentrell told him. "For Black History Month this year, our classroom assignment is Imagine Life Without African American Inventors."

"Ummm, Black people invented stuff, Mr. Kentrell?" Eric questioned.

"Of course, they did," Mr. Kentrell answered. "Who can name something an African American invented?"

"Garrett Morgan invented the traffic signal," said Toni. "That's how people can drive safely."

"You are right," Mr. Kentrell told her. "Who else?"

"Lyda D. Newman invented the hairbrush," replied Michael.

"John Lee Love invented the pencil sharpener," Jack stated.

"I know Sarah Goode was the first African American woman to receive a United States patent for the invention of a folding cabinet bed," Shelly said. "And Annie Malone is one of the first African American women to become a millionaire. Women rule!"

"Yes, yes, yes. You are all correct," Mr. Kentrell said with a smile. "As you can see, we have evolved and contributed to the invention of this great land. This year, we will focus on inventions that were created by African Americans and have shaped our everyday living. So, I want everyone to research one inventor to tell us about at our Black History assembly. See you all tomorrow.

"Daddy! Daddy!" Michelle yelled as she walked in the house.

"Yes, babygirl. I'm right here. What's wrong?" he asked.

"Dad, I have to research African American inventors. Can you help me?" Michelle said.

"Sure," her dad replied. "There are things right here in this room that African American inventors created. Can you guess three?"

"African American people invented stuff in this house?" Michelle asked while looking around.

Walking out of the kitchen, her mother replied, "They sure did."

"I have no clue," Michelle told them.

"Well, that cellphone you use was made possible because of the gamma-electric cell invented by Henry Sampson in 1971. His cell allowed radio waves to transmit and receive audio signals. Then there's this lamp that exists because of Michael Harvey, who invented the lantern lamp. Marie Van Brittan Brown invented the home security system. If it weren't for her invention, we nor our personal belongings in here would be safe."

"Wow! African Americans invented and contributed all of that?" Michelle said.

"Let's not forget our mail would be on the ground if it weren't for Philip B. Downing, who invented the street letter box," Michelle's mother told her. "Nowadays, we call it a mailbox."

"Plus, we wouldn't have doors with knobs if it weren't for Osbourn Dorsey, who received a patent for the improvements on a door-closing device," her dad added.

"Why don't we learn this stuff in school?" Michelle asked. "These textbooks will have you believe that we were only slaves fighting for freedom. There is greatness that comes from our ancestors."

"Michelle, textbooks do not tell everything," her dad replied. "They don't share every part of our history and contribution. That's why it's important to read books other than textbooks, watch documentaries that teach our history, and share the stories of the past so we know just how important we are to America. Slavery is what brought us here," he continued, "but our ability to evolve this land makes us valuable. We may not always get credit for the things we've done, but if we know our story, we can celebrate our legacy as a people."

"I AM PROUD TO BE AN AFRICAN AMERICAN!" MICHELLE SAID.

Good morning, boys and girls," Principal Imani said. "Welcome to our Black History Month assembly. Your teachers have told me that you all worked extremely hard on your assignments, and I can't wait to learn more about the African American contributions to America."

"First up, we will have Mr. Kentrell's class, who is going to share their presentation Imagine Life Without African American Inventors."

"Greetings, everyone!" Mr. Kentrell started. "African Americans have a huge hand in the growth and evolution of this great country. For this year's Black History Month, my class learned about all the amazing inventions by African Americans that we use today — from appliances, medicine, electronics, and other things that make life safe and more convenient for us. Each child will present their inventor and their invention to you. First up, we will have Arlean."

"CAN YOU IMAGINE LIFE WITHOUT AFRICAN AMERICAN INVENTORS?"

More African American Inventors

Thomas Jennings ~ Dry Cleaning

Shirley Ann Jackson ~ Caller ID / Call Waiting

Benjamin Banneker ~ Wooden Clock

George Crum ~ Potato Chips

Kenneth Dunkley ~ 3D Glass

Lonnie Johnson ~ Super Soaker Gun

Dr. Mark Dean ~ Personal Computer/Computer Monitor (IBM)

John Henry Thompson ~ Lingo Language Computer Programming (used in computer and video games)

John Burr ~ Lawn Mower

John W. Butts ~ Luggage Carrier

References:

Black Inventors of the 20th and 21st Century
https://www.youtube.com/watch?v=umdq6B3HIZU, retrieved on December 6, 2020

13 African American Inventors Who Changed the World
https://www.youtube.com/watch?v=F-SmBEL2f4Y, retrieved on December 6, 2020

Morgan, Thad (2020) 8 Black Inventors Who Made Daily Life Easier. History
https://www.history.com/news/8-black-inventors-african-american
retrieved on December 6, 2020

McFadden, Christopher (2018) The A-Z List of Black Inventors. Interesting Engineering.
https://interestingengineering.com/the-a-z-list-of-black-inventors
retrieved on December 6, 2020

CPSIA information can be obtained
at www.ICGtesting.com
Printed in the USA
BVHW022347080222
628392BV00009B/337